Peace
in the Present Moment

Photographs © 2010 by Michele Penn
Foreword © 2010 by Stephen Mitchell
Design © 2010 by Hampton Roads

Byron Katie's quotes are taken from *A Thousand Names for Joy,* © 2007 Byron Katie. Reprinted with permission from Random House.

Eckhart Tolle's quotes are taken from *A New Earth*, © 2005 Eckhart Tolle. Reprinted with permission from Namaste Publishing.

Cover and text design by Tracy Johnson
Quote selection by Randy Davila and Stephen Mitchell

Hampton Roads Publishing Company, Inc.
Charlottesville, VA 22906
www.hrpub.com

Library of Congress Cataloging-in-Publication data available upon request.

ISBN: 978-1-57174-643-6

Manufactured in Hong Kong
GWP
10 9 8 7 6 5 4 3 2 1

Peace

in the Present Moment

Selected Quotations from

Eckhart Tolle and **Byron Katie**

Foreword by **Stephen Mitchell** Photographs by **Michele Penn**

The teachings of Eckhart Tolle and Byron Katie have had a profound impact on me both professionally as well as personally. The following quotes from *A New Earth* and *A Thousand Names for Joy* are some of my favorites.

While photographing the innermost details of the flower, I am in awe of the beauty that is inherent in its stillness, and reminded of the peace that exists only in the present moment.

As you look through this book, please know that none of my photos are enhanced or edited in any way. My goal is to show you the true being that is the flower, exactly as nature has gifted it.

With peace and love,
Michele Penn

In *Peace in the Present Moment*, Michele Penn's stunning photographs add color and light to the wisdom of Eckhart Tolle (noted in the book as ET) and Byron Katie (noted in the book as BK). The quotes that make up this book are excerpted from Eckhart Tolle's *A New Earth: Awakening to Your Life's Purpose*, and Byron Katie's *A Thousand Names for Joy: Living in Harmony with the Way Things Are.* Stephen Mitchell adds an eloquent discussion of the flower as a symbol for enlightenment. It is our privilege to combine these four points of view into one volume.

"People from a planet without flowers would think we must be mad with joy the whole time to have the things about us."

–*Iris Murdoch*

There is an old Zen legend called "The Flower Sermon." A large audience of monks was gathered in front of the Buddha one morning, waiting for him to begin his sermon. Time passed, but he just sat there without saying a word. Finally, the Buddha picked up a flower and held it out to the audience. No one understood, except for one monk, Mahakashyapa, who smiled.

What did he understand? Ah, that's the big question, isn't it? If the Buddha had held up a turnip, or a dog turd, would Mahakashyapa still have understood? Would his smile have been the same one that blossomed at the sight of the flower? Or is there something particularly enlightening about flowers, something that allows us to see heaven in them, as Blake said, and eternity contained in an hour, a moment?

The Buddhists talk about "suchness"—the fact that everything is just the way it is, the delight that everything is as it is. This may sound rather mystical, but "suchness" is the least mystical concept in the world. It's not even a concept: as soon as it becomes one, it's worthless. It's a pointer, to the flowerness of flowers, the smileness of smiles, the silent, inexpressible pleasure of understanding that nothing needs to be understood. Look, a flower. How gorgeous, how grace-filled and grace-bestowing! Oh: what did you say it was?

Biologists tell us that flowers are the reproductive organs of flowering plants—which thickens the plot, in case we need our plot any thicker. These small, motionless beings are, as they are out of a desire to re-create themselves, using all possible means—color, shape, smell, trickery of every kind—to attract other small beings, capable of motion, to pollinate them so that their beauty can go on forever, or at least for another few hundred million years. The pollinators come, we are told, in the guises of wind, water, bees, birds, bats, even pygmy possums. Thus the marvelous dance of attraction and propagation dances itself on, each flower a princess waiting in her golden tower for a mobile prince to find her, a fuzzy or feathered god to swoop down and leave in an untidy rush of fulfillment.

Sexuality is what it's all about, you might say. Flowers positively drip with it, and their beauty is simply a way of getting themselves handed down to future generations. You might say that the whole point of a flower is the seed, if it weren't equally true that the whole point of a seed is the flower. Which came first: the chicken or the egg? Fortunately, we don't have to decide. Planning, neediness, deviousness, devotion: all take place in perfect innocence, since (as far as we know) the flower is unaware of what it is doing and of why it is doing it. It simply says to the susceptible passing honeybee or bird, "Look at me, smell me, come to me: how beautiful I am!" This would be pure selfishness if there were any ego in it.

The flower is a traditional symbol not only of sexuality, but of enlightenment—and there is an appropriateness to this. The act of self-realization feels like a blossoming of a clarity previously unsuspected. Its seeds go far. In this sense, understanding is the flower, and someone like Eckhart Tolle or Byron Katie is the bee, or the bird, drinking the nectar of self-awareness and serenely flying away with pollen-encrusted legs. The pollen can take the form of words such as the ones included in the book you are about to read. Those of you who find yourselves inspired are encouraged to go deeper by exploring *A Thousand Names for Joy* and *A New Earth*.

Ultimately, though, there is no such thing as a symbol, because all things are simply themselves. Flowers are not sex, they are not enlightenment, they are just flowers. Bees are just bees. Words are just words, which can point to a reality beyond themselves and beyond us. Eckhart Tolle and Byron Katie each woke up in one moment from the glittering, deadly dreams of the ego. They found themselves, to their unspeakable joy, unfurling like flowers under the spacious heaven of the mind, or, more accurately, they found themselves as flower, bee, soil, sky—the whole kit and caboodle—perfect just as they are. That understanding belongs to you as well.

Stephen Mitchell
Valentine's Day, 2010

Like the Taoist sages of ancient China, Jesus likes to draw our attention to nature because he sees a power at work in it that humans have lost touch with. It is the creative power of the universe. Jesus goes on to say that if God clothes simple flowers in such beauty, how much more will God clothe you. That is to say, that while nature is a beautiful expression of the evolutionary impulse of the universe, when humans become aligned with the intelligence that underlies it, they will express that same impulse on a higher, more wondrous level. **ET**

There is a perfection beyond what the unquestioned mind can know. You can count on it to take you wherever you need to be, whenever you need to be there, and always exactly on time. When mind understands that it is just the reflection of the nameless intelligence that has created the whole apparent universe, it is filled with delight. It delights that it is everything, it delights that it is nothing, it delights that it is brilliantly kind and free of all identity, free to be its unlimited, unstoppable, unimaginable life. It dances in the light of its own understanding that nothing has ever happened, and that everything that has ever happened—everything that ever *can* happen—is good. **BK**

Reality is a unified whole, but thought cuts it up into fragments. This gives rise to fundamental misperceptions, for example, that there are separate things and events, or that this *is the cause of* that. *Every thought implies a perspective, and every perspective, by its very nature, implies limitation, which ultimately means that it is not true, at least not absolutely.* ET

The only time you suffer is when you believe a thought that argues with reality. You are the cause of your own suffering—but only all of it. There is no suffering in the world; there's only an uninvestigated story that leads you to believe it. There is no suffering in the world that's real. Isn't that amazing! BK

If you don't become speechless when looking out into space on a clear night, you are not really looking, not aware of the totality of what is there. You are probably only looking at the objects and perhaps seeking to name them. If you have ever experienced a sense of awe when looking into space, perhaps even felt a deep reverence in the face of this incomprehensible mystery, it means you must have relinquished for a moment your desire to explain and label and have become aware not only of the objects in space but of the infinite depth of space itself. You must have become still enough inside to notice the vastness in which these countless worlds exist. The feeling of awe is not derived from the fact that there are billions of worlds out there, but the depth that contains them all. ET

Reality—the way that it is, exactly as it is, in every moment—is always kind. It's our *story* about reality that blurs our vision, obscures what's true, and leads us to believe that there is injustice in the world. I sometimes say that you move totally away from reality when you believe that there is a legitimate reason to suffer. When you believe that any suffering is legitimate, you become the champion of suffering, the perpetuator of it in yourself. It's insane to believe that suffering is caused by anything outside the mind. A clear mind doesn't suffer. That's not possible. **BK**

The most important, the primordial relationship in your life is your relationship with the Now, or rather with whatever form the Now takes, that is to say, what is or what happens. If your relationship with the Now is dysfunctional, that dysfunction will be reflected in every relationship and every situation you encounter. The ego could be defined simply in this way: a dysfunctional relationship with the present moment. It is at this moment that you can decide what kind of relationship you want to have with the present moment. ET

People are fascinated with the origin of things. "When did the universe begin?" they ask. "Where do I come from?" The answers to questions like these are obvious once you get a little clarity. When did the universe begin? Right now (if at all). A clear mind sees that any past is just a thought. There's no proof for the validity of any thought other than another thought, and even *that* thought is gone, and then the thought "That thought is gone" is itself gone. There is only now, and even "now" is a thought of the past. Actually, the universe has no beginning and no end. It's constantly beginning, and it's always over. Where do I come from? From this very thought. Oops: now I'm gone. **BK**

Everything seems to be subject to time, yet it all happens in the Now. That is the paradox. Wherever you look, there is plenty of circumstantial evidence for the reality of time—a rotting apple, your face in the bathroom mirror compared to your face in a photo taken thirty years ago—yet you never find any direct evidence, you never experience time itself. You only ever experience the present moment, or rather what happens in it. If you go by direct evidence only, then there is no time, and the Now is all there ever is. ET

The I is the origin of the whole universe. All thought is born out of that first thought, and the I cannot exist without these thoughts. Every story of enlightenment is gone. It's just one more story about the past. If it happened five seconds ago, it might as well have been a million years. The thoughts are what allow the I to believe that it has an identity. When you see that, you see that there's no you to be enlightened. You stop believing in yourself as an identity, and you become equal to everything. **BK**

When freedom from ego is your goal for the future, you give yourself more time, and more time means more ego. Look carefully to find out if your spiritual search is a disguised form of ego. Even trying to get rid of your "self" can be a disguised search for more if the getting rid of your "self" is made into a future goal. Giving yourself more time is precisely this: giving your "self" more time. ET

The more limited, the more narrowly egoic the view of yourself, the more you will see, focus on, and react to the egoic limitations, the unconsciousness in others. Their "faults," or what you perceive as their faults, become to you their identity. This means you will see only the ego in them and thus strengthen the ego in yourself. Instead of looking "through" the ego in others, you are looking "at" the ego. Who is looking at the ego? The ego in you. ET

Sanity doesn't suffer, ever. A clear mind is beautiful and sees only its own reflection. It bows in humility to itself; it falls at its own feet. It doesn't add anything or subtract anything; it simply knows the difference between what's real and what's not. And because of this, danger isn't a possibility. A lover of what is looks forward to everything: life, death, disease, loss, earthquakes, bombs, anything the mind might be tempted to call "bad." Life will bring us everything we need, to show us what we haven't undone yet. Nothing outside ourselves can make us suffer. Except for our unquestioned thoughts, every place is paradise. BK

Why did anxiety, stress, or negativity arise? Because you turned away from the present moment. And why did you do that? You thought something else was more important. You forgot your main purpose. One small error, one misperception, creates a world of suffering. ET

In my experience, confusion is the only suffering. Confusion is when you argue with what is. When you're perfectly clear, what is is what you want. So when you want something that's different from what is, you can know that you're very confused. BK

When you hate what you are doing, complain about your surroundings, curse things that are happening or have happened, or when your internal dialogue consists of shoulds and shouldn'ts, of blaming and accusing, then you are arguing with what is, arguing with that which is already the case. You are making Life into an enemy and Life says, "War is what you want, and war is what you get." External reality, which always reflects back to you your inner state, is then experienced as hostile. ET

When you understand that you're one with reality, you don't seek, because you realize that what you have is what you want. Everything makes sense, because you don't superimpose your thinking onto reality. And when you make a mistake, you realize immediately that it wasn't a mistake; it was what should have happened, because it happened. Before the fact, there were infinite possibilities; after the fact, there was only one. The more clearly you realize that *would have, could have, should have* are just unquestioned thoughts, the more you can appreciate the value of that apparent mistake and what it produced. Seeing this is forgiveness in its totality. In the clarity of understanding, forgiveness is unnecessary. **BK**

When forms that you had identified with, that gave you your sense of self, collapse or are taken away, it can lead to a collapse of the ego, since ego is identification with form. When there is nothing to identify with anymore, who are you? When forms around you die or death approaches, your sense of Beingness, of I Am, is freed from its entanglement with form: Spirit is released from its imprisonment in matter. You realize your essential identity as formless, as an all-pervasive Presence, of Being prior to all forms, all identifications. You realize your true identity as consciousness itself, rather than what consciousness had identified with. That's the peace of God. The ultimate truth of who you are is not I am this or I am that, but I Am. ET

Inquiry always leaves you with less of a story. Who would you be without your story? You never know until you inquire. There is no story that is you or that leads to you. Every story leads away from you. You are what exists before all stories. You are what remains when the story is understood. **BK**

I don't know what's best for me or you or the world. I don't try to impose my will on you or on anyone else. I don't want to change you or improve you or convert you or help you or heal you. I just welcome things as they come and go. That's true love. The best way of leading people is to let them find their own way. **BK**

Nobody can tell you who you are. It would just be another concept, so it would not change you. Who you are requires no belief. In fact, every belief is an obstacle. It does not even require your realization, since you already are who you are. But without realization, who you are does not shine forth into this world. **ET**

The joy of Being, which is the only true happiness, cannot come to you through any form, possession, achievement, person, or event—through anything that happens. That joy cannot come to you—ever. It emanates from the formless dimension within you, from consciousness itself and thus is one with who you are. ET

The litmus test for self-realization is a constant state of gratitude. This gratitude is not something you can look for or find. It comes from another direction, and it takes you over completely. It's so vast that it can't be dimmed or overlaid. The short version would be "mind in love with itself." It's the total acceptance and consumption of itself reflected back at the same moment in the central place that is like fusion. When you live your life from that place of gratitude, you've come home. **BK**

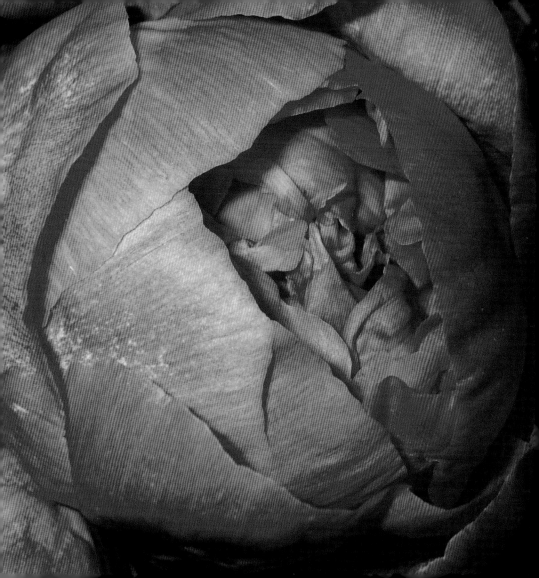

You can't let go of a stressful thought, because you didn't create it in the first place. A thought just appears. You're not doing it. You can't let go of what you have no control over. Once you've questioned the thought, you don't let go of it, *it* lets go of *you.* It no longer means what you thought it meant. The world changes, because the mind that projected it has changed. Your whole life changes, and you don't even care, because you realize that you already have everything you need. **BK**

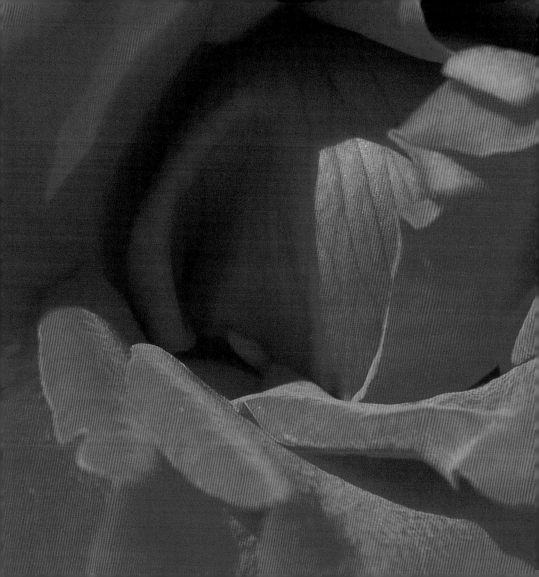

Once you see and accept the transience of all things and the inevitability of change, you can enjoy the pleasures of the world while they last without fear of loss or anxiety about the future. When you are detached, you gain a higher vantage point from which to view the events in your life instead of being trapped inside them. You become like an astronaut who sees the planet Earth surrounded by the vastness of space and realizes a paradoxical truth: The earth is precious and at the same time insignificant. ET

At some point in their lives, most people become aware that there is not only birth, growth, success, good health, pleasure, and winning, but also loss, failure, sickness, old age, decay, pain, and death. Conventionally these are labeled "good" and "bad," order and disorder. The "meaning" of people's lives is usually associated with what they term the "good," but the good is continually threatened by collapse, breakdown, disorder; threatened by meaninglessness and the "bad," when explanations fail and life ceases to make sense. Sooner or later, disorder will irrupt into everyone's life no matter how many insurance policies he or she has. It may come in the form of loss or accident, sickness, disability, old age, death. However, the irruption of disorder into a person's life, and the resultant collapse of a mentally defined meaning, can become the opening into a higher order. ET

No one knows what's good and what's bad. No one knows what death is. Maybe it's not a something; maybe it's not even a nothing. It's the pure unknown, and I love that. We imagine that death is a state of being or a state of nothingness, and we frighten ourselves with our own concepts. I'm a lover of what is: I love sickness and health, coming and going, life and death. I see life and death as equal. Reality is good; so death must be good, whatever it is, if it's anything at all. **BK**

If peace is really what you want, then you will choose peace. If peace mattered to you more than anything else and if you truly knew yourself to be spirit rather than the little me, you would remain nonreactive and absolutely alert when confronted with challenging people or situations. You would immediately accept the situation and thus become one with it rather than separate yourself from it. Then out of your alertness would come a response. Who you are (consciousness), not who you think you are (a small me), would be responding. It would be powerful and effective and would make no person or situation into an enemy. ET

Life is simple. Everything happens *for* you, not *to* you. Everything happens at exactly the right moment, neither too soon nor too late. You don't have to like it—it's just easier if you do. If you have a problem, it can only be because of your unquestioned thinking. **BK**

To be in alignment with what is *means to be in a relationship of inner nonresistance with what happens. It means not to label it mentally as good or bad, but to let it be. Does this mean you can no longer take action to bring about change in your life? On the contrary. When the basis for your actions is inner alignment with the present moment, your actions become empowered by the intelligence of Life itself.* **ET**

I've heard people say that they cling to their painful thoughts because they're afraid that without them they wouldn't be activists for peace. "If I felt completely peaceful," they say, "why would I bother taking action at all?" My answer is "Because that's what love does." To think that we need sadness or outrage to motivate us to do what's right is insane. As if the clearer and happier you get, the less kind you become. As if when someone finds freedom, she just sits around all day with drool running down her chin. My experience is the opposite. Love is action. It's clear, it's kind, it's effortless, and it's irresistible. **BK**

There's nothing you can do with love. All you can do is experience it. That's as intimate as you can ever be with another human being. You can hug him, you can kiss him, you can pack him up, take him home, cuddle him, feed him, give him your money, give him your life—and that's not it. Love is nothing you can demonstrate or prove. It's what you are. It's not a doing, it can't be "done," it's too vast to do anything with. As you open to the experience of love, it will kill who you think you are. It will have no other. It will kill anything in its way. **BK**

No name, no thought, can possibly be true in an ultimate sense. It's all provisional; it's all changing. The dark, the nameless, the unthinkable—that is what you can absolutely trust. It doesn't change, and it's benevolent. When you realize this, you just have to laugh. There's nothing serious about life or death. **BK**

To awaken within the dream is our purpose now. When we are awake within the dream, the ego-created earth drama comes to an end and a more benign and wondrous dream arises. This is the new earth. ET

The collective disease of humanity is that people are so engrossed in what happens, so hypnotized by the world of fluctuating forms, so absorbed in the content of their lives, they have forgotten the essence, that which is beyond content, beyond form, beyond thought. They are so consumed by time that they have forgotten eternity, which is their origin, their home, their destiny. Eternity is the living reality of who you are. **ET**

I love that what is of true value can't be seen or heard. It's nothing and it's everything, it's nowhere and it's right under your nose—it *is* your nose, as a matter of fact, along with everything else. It can't be reached or achieved, because as soon as you start looking for it, you leave it. It doesn't have to be achieved, only noticed. Nothing anyone says is true, and no thought that arises within you is true. There's nothing. And yet, here is the world again. The sun in the sky. The sidewalk. The dog trotting along on a leash. **BK**

The great arises out of small things that are honored and cared for. Everybody's life really consists of small things. Greatness is mental abstraction and a favorite fantasy of the ego. The paradox is that the foundation for greatness is honoring the small things of the present moment instead of pursuing the idea of greatness. The present moment is always small in the sense that it is always simple, but concealed within it lies the greatest power. Like the atom, it is one of the smallest things yet contains enormous power. ET

There's no mistake, and there's nothing lacking. We're always going to get what we need, not what we *think* we need. Then we come to see that what we need is not only what we have, it's what we want. Then we come to want only what is. That way we always succeed, whatever happens. BK

Behind the sometimes seemingly random or even chaotic succession of events in our lives as well as in the world lies concealed the unfolding of a higher order and purpose. This is beautifully expressed in the Zen saying "The snow falls, each flake in its appropriate place." We can never understand this higher order through thinking about it because whatever we think about is content; whereas, the higher order emanates from the formless realm of consciousness, from universal intelligence. But we can glimpse it, and more than that, align ourselves with it, which means be conscious participants in the unfolding of that higher purpose. **ET**

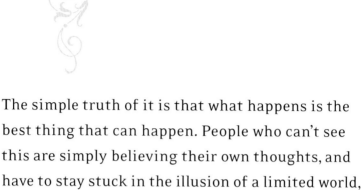

The simple truth of it is that what happens is the best thing that can happen. People who can't see this are simply believing their own thoughts, and have to stay stuck in the illusion of a limited world, lost in the war with what is. It's a war they'll always lose, because it argues with reality, and reality is always benevolent. When you argue with reality, you lose—but only 100 percent of the time. BK